Teacher's Book

MORE! 4

Ulrike Kamauf · Günter Gerngross
Herbert Puchta · Christian Holzmann

Teil B: Worksheets

W0320184

HELBLING LANGUAGES

Enriched course

MORE! 4 TEACHER'S BOOK – TEIL B
ENRICHED COURSE

by
Ulrike Kamauf
Günter Gerngross
Herbert Puchta
Christian Holzmann

www.helblinglanguages.at

Design and layout by Pixarte

Printed by Athesia

First published 2010

Second edition 2011, fourth print run 2016

ISBN 978-3-85272-215-3

Acknowledgements
Illustrated by Giovanni Da Re, Valentina Baldisserotto Mai, Björn Pertoft, Lorenzo Sabbatini.

The publisher would like to thank the following for their kind permission to reproduce the following photographs:

Alamy p21, p44; **Bloomsbury** cover image of Harry Potter and the Half-Blood Prince by J.K. Rowling p50; **David Loftus** p25 (Jamie Oliver); **Dreamstime** p7 (friends having a barbecue; family having a picnic), p17 (Celtics), p33 (Kakadu National Park), p54; **HarpersCollins Publishers** cover image of Millions by Frank Cottrell Boyce, cover art © by Twentieth Century Fox Film Corporation p50; **Helbling Languages** p42; © **iStockphoto** p4, p12, p30, p33 (Alice Springs), p36, p38, p40 (ticket; diary), p41, p46, p56; **Shutterstock** p7, p13, p16, p17, p22, p26, p28, p31, p32, p33, p35, p37, p40, p43, p45, p47, p59; The Random House **Group Ltd** cover images of Noughts and crosses by Malorie Blackman, The curious incident of the dog in the night-time by Mark Haddon p50; **WARNER BROS/DC COMICS / THE KOBAL COLLECTION** p30 (Superman); **Wikimedia Commons** p57.

Inhalt

Zeichenerklärung
- ● leichte Aufgabenstellung
- ■ Aufgabenstellung mittleren Schwierigkeitsgrades
- ★ anspruchsvolle Aufgabenstellung

Worksheet 1

1 Fill in the past simple or the past continuous.

Anna's job interview

Do you remember Anna from Denmark? (If not, go to your Student's Book, p. 8.) In the interview she also told the interviewer about the first time she met the family she is working for, the Morgans. Here is part of the interview.

I: Anna, you are working as an au pair at the moment, aren't you?

A: Yes, I am and I really love my job. From eight in the morning till five in the afternoon I look after Liam and Michael, they're four-year-old twins. I was really surprised to get the job because of what happened on my first day in Dublin …

I: What went wrong? Tell me.

A: Well, I [1] ......had...... (have) a job interview with the Morgans, first thing in the morning at nine. I [2] ......was staying...... (stay) at a small hotel which is quite a long way from the Morgans' flat. So I [3] ......decided...... (decide) to go by bus and LUAS.

I: LUAS … what's that?

A: It's a new tram system in Dublin; I think it's OK, but there are only two lines. Anyway, while I [4] ......was waiting...... (wait) at the bus stop this morning, the crowd [5] ......was slowly getting...... (slowly, get) bigger and bigger. I [6] ......asked...... (ask) a man why the bus [7] ......was running...... (run) late and he [8] ......told...... (tell) me that this [9] ......happened...... (happen) all the time. I [10] ......tried...... (try) to phone the family but nobody [11] ......answered...... (answer) the phone. When I finally [12] ......arrived...... (arrive) at the Morgans' place, it [13] ......was...... (be) ten o'clock. Mrs Morgan [14] ......was already waiting...... (already, wait) for me. I thought that I would never get this job. But everything was fine in the end and she told me that she had been late for her first job interview as well. If there's one thing I really hate about Dublin, it's the public transport. It takes a long time and isn't reliable* at all.

VOCABULARY
reliable – verlässlich

nach SB p. 08

Worksheet 2

UNIT 1

● 1 **Circle the correct form: past simple or past continuous.**

A school trip to Glendalough

Linda, a 14-year-old British student, and her classmates took a trip to Glendalough last month. This is what she wrote in her diary.

On our way there, Mr Miller [1]**told / was telling** *us some interesting things about Glendalough. I* [2]**tried / was trying** *to listen to what he said, but I couldn't. While he* [3]**explained / was explaining** *the history of the place, the boys who* [4]**sat / were sitting** *in the back of the bus* [5]**talked / were talking** *all the time. Not only that, they* [6]**also sang / were also singing** *stupid songs. That* [7]**was / was being** *a real pain! When we* [8]**got off / were getting off** *the bus, we* [9]**went / were going** *for a short hike around one of the lakes. What a beautiful place! I* [10]**was taking / took** *lots of photos. Back on the bus, Mr Miller* [11]**noticed / was noticing** *that one of the boys, Tommy,* [12]**missed / was missing**. *While the bus driver and Mr Miller* [13]**searched / were searching** *for him, we* [14]**looked / were looking** *at each other's photos. After an hour Tommy finally* [15]**appeared / was appearing**. *Now he isn't allowed to go out on his own any more. Serves him right!*

Worksheet 3

★ 1 **Read Molly's blog again in your Workbook on p. 4. In her blog, Molly asks for advice because she would like to travel to Ireland soon. Imagine that you have just spent two weeks in Ireland. In your text, give her a few tips for her trip to Ireland. Write about:**

- the places you liked most;
- the people you met;
- an exciting adventure you had during your stay.

2 **Read the story on p. 10 in your Student's Book again. Here is how the story continues:**

An Irish story

"Will you marry me, Mary?" the young farmer asked. Mary laughed. "Yes, I will," she said. And she thought: "Then the small bag *and* the big one will be mine!"
Shortly after they were married, the young farmer had to go to town again. That evening Mary couldn't fall asleep, so she started reading a book in bed. Suddenly the ghost appeared in front of the bedroom window. The ghost was waving at Mary …

What happened next? Go on. Write 100 – 150 words and choose a title for your story.

....

....

....

....

....

....

....

....

....

....

....

Worksheet 4

UNIT 1

● 1 **Write sentences about Christopher's Sunday. Use the past continuous and make sentences about his friends and family.**

Christopher's Sunday

Last Sunday, Christopher got up late. His parents and younger brother had already left early because they wanted to take a long walk in the woods. He didn't have any plans for the day so Christopher phoned his friends. But none of them was at home.

Oliver was not at home because he ... .

....

....

....

....

....

....

Worksheet 1

UNIT 2

■ 1 **Use the words in the box to complete the newspaper article.**

witness
murder
blackmail
evidence
weapon
victim
murderer

THE LONDON MORNING PAPER

Dead body found in the Thames

Saturday evening, around 7 p.m., the police were told about a suspicious* body floating on the River Thames. Shortly after that, a woman called the police again. She said that she had taken her dog for a walk along the river, throwing a stick for her dog to get it. As she was waiting for her dog, she suddenly noticed a dead body that was caught in the branches of a tree close to the bank of the river.

The police are now sure that it was 1.......................... . The man had not fallen into the river by accident, he had been shot from behind and had been thrown into the Thames. The 2.........................., probably a 9 mm gun, has not been found yet.

First, there wasn't any 3.......................... that might tell the police who the murderer was. But fortunately, the 4.......................... had had his wallet in the inside pocket of his jacket. His name was Roger Frampton, 55. When the police searched his flat, they found a letter. Somebody had tried to 5.......................... him. The circumstances* will be reported to the public soon and this will eventually* help them to arrest the 6.......................... . As of now, the woman who was walking her dog is still the only 7.......................... .

VOCABULARY
suspicious – verdächtig
circumstances – Umstände
eventually – schlussendlich

★ 2 **What happened next? Write the newspaper article. The police investigated the crime and finally arrested somebody.**

The following questions should help you write your newspaper article (200 words):

- Who blackmailed Roger Frampton? What were the motives?
- What did the letter say?
- When was he shot?
- How did the murderer(s) take him to the river? …

  ▶ nach SB p. 18

Worksheet 2

★ 1 **Write an interview and/or a report.**

Another murder mystery

On September 5th, Joel Hunter was found dead in a hotel room in Miami, Florida. Mr Hunter had been one of two owners of Netcorp, a huge computer company in Chicago. He had been on a business trip when the murder happened.

Here is a list of people who joined him on his trip:

- Catherine Hunter: his wife; they shared the same hotel room
- David Brooks: his business partner, who owns half of the company
- Tom Atkinson: his assistant
- John Gibbs: the lawyer of the company

The day of the murder, Joel Hunter had left his wife and the three men after lunch. He said that he was very tired and wanted a short rest. When his wife went looking after him two hours later, she found him dead in their room. There was a wound in his stomach. All the windows were closed. (They couldn't be opened because of the air conditioning* at the hotel.) A wallet and some documents were scattered* on the floor. Mrs Hunter was the only person who had a key to the room. Now Inspector Packard is investigating the crime. He is questioning the suspects.

a Choose one of the four suspects above and write Inspector Packard's interview with him/her.

b Write Inspector Packard's final report in which he explains who the murderer was and what his/her motives were.

VOCABULARY
air conditioning – Klimaanlage
scattered – verstreut

Worksheet 3

1 Complete the sentences with the past or the past perfect form of the verbs.

When I [1].. (get) up in the morning, I [2].. (see) that my dog [3].. (sleep) in my bed. I [4].. (notice) that he [5].. (open) the door to my room in the night. I [6].. (not, hear) anything. That's really strange.

It [7].. (be) Sarah's birthday on Sunday. So she [8].. (organise) a huge party and [9].. (invite) all her friends. On the card it [10].. (say) that the party would start at 6 p.m. I [11].. (be) a bit late, but when I finally [12].. (walk) into Sarah's living room I saw lots of presents which people [13].. (put) on a table next to the buffet. I suddenly [14].. (remember) that I [15].. (leave) her birthday present at home! So I [16].. (decide) to leave quietly and go home to get it as quickly as possible.

Henry [17].. (must see) the doctor yesterday. He told the doctor what [18].. (happen) two days ago. He [19].. (meet) his friends who always [20].. (practise) new jumps on their skateboards after school. But Henry [21].. (fall) and [22].. (land) on his face. When Henry [23].. (wake) up the next morning, his left eye [24].. (be) black and blue.

Worksheet 4

1 Circle the correct words in past or past perfect.

Read what went wrong for Christopher yesterday:

"In the morning I [1] **was / had been** late because I [2] **didn't set / hadn't set** the alarm clock the night before. On the bus I [3] **had to sit / had had to sit** next to Jenny because all the other places [4] **were taken / had been taken**. At school I [5] **was / had been** hungry because I [6] **didn't eat / hadn't eaten** anything for breakfast. I [7] **wasn't able / hadn't been able** to open the door of my cupboard because I [8] **forgot / had forgotten** my key at home. I couldn't do the exercise in the English lesson because I [9] **didn't finish / hadn't finished** the book we should have read. My football team [10] **had / had had** a match in the afternoon and we [11] **played / had played** really badly. After the match we [12] **were / had been** quite angry because we [13] **didn't score / hadn't scored** a goal and the other team [14] **won / had won**. When I finally [15] **got / had got** home in the evening, my family [16] **had / had had** dinner without me and my sister [17] **ate / had eaten** my dessert. Well, tomorrow's another day. I hope I won't forget to set the alarm clock again …"

Worksheet I

■ 1 **Read the following parts of the interview with Annabel. What did she tell the interviewer? Put the words in order to make sentences.**

Annabel speaks out

1 "I've always wanted to become a journalist.

That's / to / me / for / parents / why / hard / my / study / want / school."

....

2 "I always listen to people and their problems. Then I write articles about them.

more / I / my / to / want / tolerant / be / readers."

....

3 "Last week two teenagers organised a protest.

They / local / new / stop / to / wanted / a / motorway project / people."

....

4 "Kids working for Headliners want the readers to think about teenagers' problems.

to / them / They / understand / problems / want / these."

....

5 "Many kids around the world don't have a good life.

us / want / to / better / them / I / make / place / world / for / a / the."

....

6 "It's really important to speak out.

also / stand / you / up / want / rights / for / your / I / to!"

....

  ▶ nach SB p. 23

Worksheet 2

■ 1 a **Fill in the missing connecting ideas where they belong.**

Is it over?

Do you remember Stevie and Rachel?
Look at their story again (Student's Book p. 25).
Rachel doesn't know what to do any more,
so she decides to write a letter to you and ask
for your advice. Here is Rachel's letter.
Read it carefully.

so that
however
because of
although

Hi,

I've fallen in love with Stevie, a boy I met at a friend's party. We've been seeing each other for more than a month now and things have been going really well ... until my family's garden party last Saturday. Stevie was not really looking forward to it in the first place. At the party he was talking to my cousins, the twins. And then, suddenly, he was gone! We haven't talked to each other since then 1................................ *I miss him very much. He sent me a long email, explaining that he didn't feel comfortable at the garden party* 2................................ *the twins who were making fun of his clothes. Stevie thinks that it's a problem that my family is rather rich and lives in a better neighbourhood than his. He says that my mum and dad don't like him* 3................................ *it might really be a problem for our relationship. Mum and dad,* 4................................*, think that he's OK.*

I know that we should talk – I just can't see his problem. And as for the stupid twins, he should have just laughed about them. What can I tell him now? I don't want to lose him. Please help me!

Yours,
Rachel

★ b **Write an answer in about 120 – 150 words. Tell Rachel what you think about the situation and what she should do.**

Worksheet 3

■ 1 **What do they want them to do? Make sentences.**

1

2

3

4

5

6

▶ nach SB p. 27

Worksheet 4

★ **1 Write a letter of 180 – 200 words to an Agony Aunt.**

Imagine the following situation: A girl in your class is bullied every day by some of your classmates. They make fun of her looks, her good marks at school and her hobbies (playing the piano and writing poetry).

You have tried to help the girl but the bullying won't stop. Describe the situation to the Agony Aunt and ask what you can do to help your desperate* classmate and stop the bullying.

VOCABULARY
desperate – verzweifelt

★ **2 You have read about Annabel and her work for the online magazine Headliners (Student's Book p. 26). Choose one of the ideas below and write a letter of 120 – 180 words to Annabel in which you talk about the things you would like to change. Describe the situation and say how you would like to change it.**

- too much work for school
- bullies in the classroom
- teenagers hanging out with their bikes in front of the school

● **3 What do people want YOU to do? Write at least six sentences and say what**

- your teachers
- your parents
- your friends

want you to do.

....

....

....

....

....

....

■ 1 **Read the text and tick T (*True*) or F (*False*).**

*Make Way for Ducklings** – The story of a children's book from Boston

Make Way for Ducklings is a famous picture book for children which was written and illustrated* by Robert McCloskey in 1941.
The story begins with two ducks, Mr and Mrs Mallard, looking for a place to raise a family. They spend the night at the Public Garden Lagoon in Boston. When Mrs Mallard is nearly killed by a biker in the park the following morning, the ducks fly away and land on an island in the Charles River. They meet a policeman named Michael who feeds them every day. Soon after, Mrs Mallard hatches* eight ducklings. Mr Mallard takes a trip along the river alone while Mrs Mallard raises the ducklings in the meantime. They decide to meet a week later at the Boston Public Garden. On their way there, Mrs Mallard and the ducklings are nearly killed by cars as they will not stop for them in the streets. Michael, the policeman, turns up and stops the traffic for them to cross. As they walk slowly across the city of Boston they are helped by four policemen who stop the traffic for the ducklings. This is also where the title of the book comes from. Mr Mallard is already waiting for his family in the park. They decide to stay there for the rest of their lives.
By 2010 the book had sold over two million copies. It was chosen as the official children's book of Massachusetts. The story is still very popular among children worldwide, especially for its drawings of the ducks. Every child in Boston knows the story and there is even a bronze statue of Mrs Mallard and the eight ducklings in the Public Garden of Boston. Each year there is a Duckling Day Parade for children who dress up as ducklings and ducks in spring. Bostonians seem to be really proud of this story. When you visit Boston as a tourist, you can also book a guided tour that will take you to the most famous places in the city. And guess what? Most tour buses in Boston are painted yellow and are shaped like ducks.

VOCABULARY
duckling – Entenküken, Entlein
illustrated – illustriert
hatch – ausbrüten

		T	F
1	Robert McCloskey tells the story of two ducks and their children in his book, which he also illustrated.	☐	☐
2	In the book, the policeman Michael is very fond of the ducks and feeds them every day.	☐	☐
3	On their way back into Boston, Mrs Mallard and the ducklings are nearly run over by police cars which won't stop for them.	☐	☐
4	Each year in spring, there is a Duckling Day Parade.	☐	☐
5	For his book, Robert McCloskey was elected the official children's author of Massachusetts.	☐	☐
6	Tourists in Boston can book a tour in a duck-shaped boat.	☐	☐

  ▶ nach SB p. 29

Worksheet 2

★ 1 **Read the texts. Then do the exercise below.**

Here are some entries in Janet's travel diary. The girl from England is spending her holidays with her parents and her brother Dennis in Massachusetts. They are staying with her aunt who lives in Boston.

Janet's trip to Massachusetts

Tuesday, July 20

Yesterday Aunt Patricia took us to a seafood restaurant. At first I didn't know what to eat, with all the seafood and exotic stuff on the menu. I ordered a Cape Cod Burger then, which was almost all fish. It was OK. Mum and Dennis ordered lobster because they had never eaten it before and wanted to try it. You need a special seafood cracker* in order to get the lobster's meat out. Dennis just couldn't work out how to use it and when he tried to crack the claws* open, he sent his lobster flying across the restaurant. I laughed so hard. Luckily, I took a photo of him, with the lobster on his plate. In the end, he had eaten very little and said that he would never try it again.

Wednesday, July 21

What an amazing night! I have just returned from a basketball game at the TD Garden. The Boston Celtics played against the New York Knicks – and won 92:87. It was simply awesome!! After the game we waited outside the stadium and half an hour later, the Celtics' captain turned up. He signed a Boston Celtics shirt for me – my friends won't believe it. Can hardly wait to show them!

Thursday, July 22

Cousin Jamie took me on a tour around the campus of Harvard University. She's studying law there and has to study for a difficult exam*. I've always wanted to see the university – it's in so many films and TV series. The university is not as big as I would have expected. But then Jamie told me that there are lots of different buildings and departments* all over the city, so it's actually not just one place. I took some photos and we got some books which Jamie needs for her exam from the library. Then we had some coffee at a café. It was a nice afternoon.

Write two more entries in Janet's diary. Choose from the list below which places you are going to write about. Also, write about exciting things that Janet saw/experienced there:

- a trip to the Salem Witch Museum;
- a weekend at the sea;
- an afternoon at the Public Garden;
- a concert she went to;
- a boat ride on the Charles River.

VOCABULARY
seafood cracker – Hummerzange
claws – Scheren (Greifarme des Hummers)
exam – Prüfung
departments – Abteilungen

Worksheet 3

■ **1** **Look at *The Curious Case of the Locked Room* (Unit 2). Who said what? Match the people and their statements.**

Inspector Fell

Detective Ward

Isabel Miller

Jasper Ford

Charles Dunning

Oliver Wilson

1 "I've worked in this company for forty years because I like it here. I was a friend of John Murdoch and of his father, too."

2 "I didn't kill my uncle. We went up to his office but the door was locked."

3 "I put my hand through the glass window and felt a key in the lock."

4 "We've found something in the wastepaper bin. I think you will be interested in it."

5 "It's just a spot of red wine on my jacket. If you don't believe me, you can send it to your labs and analyse it."

6 "We will call in the suspects now, Jenkins. I finally know who the murderer is."

■ **2** **Write the statements from 1 in reported speech. Use the following verbs in the past to begin your sentences.**

say
explain
tell
report
add
claim*

VOCABULARY
claim – behaupten

Worksheet 4

★ 1 **Write the sentences in reported speech.**

Part 1: The Boston Tea Party

1 Teacher: "Today Helen is going to tell us something about the Boston Tea Party."
2 Helen: "Boston was a very important place in America in the 1700s. It was an important port. Ships went in and out and took things in and out of America."
3 Helen: "About 1730 the government in Britain started to ask the Americans to pay taxes. But the Americans weren't happy about that and things weren't very good between Britain and America at that time."

....

....

....

....

....

....

....

....

Part 2: What people said at the time of the Boston Tea Party

1 The Americans: "We won't pay any money to the British any more!"
2 The Americans: "Tomorrow we're going to get on board the three ships full of tea in Boston Harbor."
3 The British: "They have taken control of our ships! They can't do that! These ships belong to us!"

....

....

....

....

....

....

....

....

Worksheet I

UNIT 5

■ 1 **Joanne has just returned from a job interview. She doesn't have a good feeling and thinks that she probably won't get the job. So many things went wrong. Now Joanne is writing about the interview in her diary. Write her text in 100 – 120 words. Choose some ideas about what went wrong from the box:**

too late (no bus) had to run heavy rain wet clothes no umbrella ran into building didn't knock at the door interrupted important meeting had to wait outside coffee spilled coffee on floor after an hour: job interview mobile phone rang chewing gum forgot important documents at home forgot what she wanted to say no eye contact …

....

....

....

....

....

....

....

....

....

....

....

....

  ▶ nach SB p. 42

Worksheet 2

■ 1 a **Write the reported questions.**

An interview with Paul Stuart, tour guide.

Two days ago, Paul Stuart was interviewed about his job as a tour guide for new teenage magazine. The following questions are taken from the interview with Paul:

1 Have you always worked as a tour guide?
2 Why is it the ideal job for you?
3 Do you sometimes get very tired in your job?
4 Have you ever experienced a dangerous situation?
5 What are your favourite countries and cities?
6 Can you recommend working as a tour guide?

1 ....
2 ....
3 ....
4 ....
5 ....
6 ....

★ b **Then write the complete interview for the website and use the following information for Paul's answers.**

1 no, bank clerk before that
2 likes meeting new people, loves travelling, never boring
3 sometimes yes, especially with large groups, not a nine to five job
4 once at a campsite: terrible thunderstorm, tents were flooded, trees blown down
5 countries – Italy, Spain; cities – Rome, Florence, Barcelona
6 absolutely yes, great challenge

1 ....
2 ....
3 ....
4 ....
5 ....
6 ....

Worksheet 3

1 **Imagine that you are taking part in a quiz about Boston. Here are the questions:**

The Boston Quiz

1 When did the Salem Witch Trials take place?
2 Why do many visitors go to Salem each year?
3 How many Americans were killed in the Boston Massacre?
4 When did the Boston Tea Party take place?
5 What's the name of Boston's most famous baseball team?
6 How often have the New England Patriots won the Super Bowl?
7 Where can people relax in Boston?
8 What special food do people often eat in restaurants in Boston?

a Write the reported questions.
Start like this: *She/He asked me …*

1 ....
2 ....
3 ....
4 ....
5 ....
6 ....
7 ....
8 ....

b Answer the questions. Check your answers with the information in your Student's Book (Unit 4). How many correct ones have you got?

1 ....
2 ....
3 ....
4 ....
5 ....
6 ....
7 ....
8 ....

  nach SB p. 43

Worksheet 4

★ a **Read the advertisement and the job application. Ian Potts saw the ad and applied for one of the jobs. Which job did he apply for?**

School leavers wanted to:

- work in a new and exciting clothes shop.
- help organise after-school activities for young children.
- help arrange local events and concerts.

Personal information			
Name	**Address**	**Telephone**	**Email**
Ian John Potts	15 Ellis Street, Bromsgrove, Worcs. WQ4 TP4	3252 1178	ianpot@hotmail.com

Qualifications and training		
date from	**to**	**School / college and qualificat**
Sept 2000	July 2006	Bromsgrove High, Pole Street, WQ2 HG1 GCSE's: Grade A – French, Maths, Biology Grade C – English, History, PE, Physics

Previous and/or present job(s) – give a summary of work you have done so far	
Place of work	**Position / responsibility**
Action Bromsgrove	Youth Leader Assistant I helped a Youth Leader to organise creative workshops for local children during their summer holidays. I also organised day trips.

Skills, ability and experience

During my summer job as an assistant youth leader, I
- used my organisational skills to organise workshops for 6 – 10 year olds.
- used my creative skills to design posters to advertise our workshops.
- used my IT skills to create a database of the children.

Additional information

I am a hard-working and energetic person. I would like a career in youth work, as I feel that I can use all my abilities in this job. My skills in IT, communication and problem-solving mean that I can be very useful to your organisation.

★ b **Apply for one of the jobs in the advertisement. Complete the form for you.**

Personal information				
Name	**Adress**	**Telephone**	**Email**	**Date of birth**

Qualifications and training		
date from	**to**	**School / college and qualifications**

Previous and/or present job(s) – give a summary of work you have done so far	
Place of work	**Position / responsibility**

Skills, ability and experience

Additional information

Worksheet I

★ **1 Complete the interview with the adjectives in the box.**

revolting
tasty
harmful
healthy
nutritious
fattening
artificial
fresh
filling

A radio interview with a chef at a school cafeteria
(I: Interviewer SR: Sam Reed)

I: Good morning and welcome to Mike's Morning Show again! With us today is Sam Reed, chef at Syracuse High School. Can you tell us a little bit about your work, Sam?

SR: Yes of course, I started working as a chef at Syracuse High three years ago. I was really shocked by the high number of overweight students there. When I saw the weekly menu, I knew why: lots of meals with too much fat, too much salt, too many sweet things. Desserts with [1]......................... flavours* and food heated in the microwave every day.

I: What did an average meal look like then? Can you give us an example?

SR: Well, mini pizzas or mini sausages for starters. Then for the main course chicken nuggets, burgers, hot dogs, always served with French fries – any kind of fast food, you name it! And for dessert a chocolate muffin or donut.

I: Why didn't the school offer [2]......................... meals?

SR: A difficult question … the kitchen staff probably hadn't ever thought about healthy options.

I: So what were the reactions when you changed the menu and introduced [3]......................... meals with natural ingredients?

SR: At first students were a bit unhappy. Soup and salad in your school dinner? Less meat? [4]......................... fruit for dessert? But it didn't take long before everybody understood the positive effects of a better diet.

I: I paid a visit to your cafeteria last week and I really have to say that the dinner tasted excellent. I had tomato soup for starters, and then fish with rice and vegetables. And the mango yoghurt for dessert was also very [5]......................... .

SR: Thanks, that's just what I wanted to show everybody. Junk food is not only [6]......................... and makes you get very fat, it's also [7]......................... and doesn't taste good at all.

I: What is your advice for our listeners? What does it take to prepare a healthy meal?

SR: Always buy fresh things. Cook simple meals; that doesn't take a long time. Broccoli pasta or rice with chicken are delicious. Don't eat microwave meals – they are usually very [8]......................... and make you feel full for a long time. Junk food is very [9]......................... to your body and your health – so try not to eat it.

I: Thank you for the interview, Sam, and thanks for talking to us today! Keep up the good work!

VOCABULARY
flavour – Geschmacksrichtung

■ **2 Mark the sentences T (*True*) or F (*False*).**

		T	F
1	Sam Reed has worked at the school cafeteria for four years now.	☐	☐
2	There were some overweight students when he started to work there.	☐	☐
3	An average meal consisted of fast food items such as mini pizzas, chicken nuggets, and donuts.	☐	☐
4	People were very happy as soon as Sam Reed started to prepare the meals at Syracuse High.	☐	☐
5	The interviewer loved the food offered at the cafeteria.	☐	☐
6	Sam Reed's advice to the listeners is not to buy fresh things and to eat microwave meals.	☐	☐

  ▶ nach SB p. 47

Worksheet 2

★ **1** **You have decided to write a letter to Jamie Oliver. Your best friend won't listen to you, so you think it's time to contact an expert. Here is the beginning of your letter:**

Dear Jamie,
I'm writing to you because I'm really worried about my best friend Chuck. He used to be really active; we were on the same swimming team. A year ago, he stopped doing sports. He said that it was getting boring and that he would like to take it easy for some time. I just couldn't believe it! We had taken part in four competitions and we had won all of them. He was an important member of our team.
Since he gave up sports, watching TV and eating have become his favourite hobbies. He spends all his time in front of the TV and when I go to see him in the afternoons, it's only films and the latest DVDs he wants to talk about. What's more, he has gained 10 kilos in the last six months. There's always lots of junk food around, empty packets of crisps, lots of chocolate, ...

Now go on. Write 140 – 160 words.
Describe Chuck's eating habits and ask for advice:
- How can you help him?
- What should your friend do?
- What should he eat to lose some of those kilos?

★ **2** **Write Jamie Oliver's answer to your letter. Write about 150 – 180 words. The following ideas may help you:**

more sports / maybe try a different sport if he is bored / ask him out for a bike tour, tennis match, etc.
eat less fattening food / talk about calorie intake with him / healthier food instead

★ **3** **Write an article for your school magazine. Write about 180 – 200 words about a project you did with your class on world hunger. Use the information in your Student's Book (p. 45).**

Write about:
- the countries where people don't have enough to eat;
- the eating habits of people in rich countries (average calorie intake, etc.);
- what we can do to help people in developing countries (collect money, organise a charity event*, etc.).

VOCABULARY
charity event – Wohltätigkeitsveranstaltung

Worksheet 3

■ 1 **Complete the sentences with the past or past perfect form of the verbs.**

Megan's job interview

"He asked me where I [1]........................ (work) before. I told him that I [2]........................ (be) a receptionist at a big hotel in the city. Then he wanted to know if I [3]........................ (like) the job there. I explained that it [4]........................ (be) OK, but that it hadn't always been pleasant when guests [5]........................ (complain) to the receptionist. I also told him that I [6]........................ (think) that it [7]........................ (be) time for a change now and that was why I [8]........................ (write) an application for the position in his company. He asked me what I [9]........................ (expect) from the job as an event manager and I told him that I [10]........................ (always, want) to work with the media and that I [11]........................ (be) good at organising events and meetings. Finally he told me that it [12]........................ (not, be) an average nine to five job and that I would have to work long hours, maybe at weekends too. I said that I [13]........................ (not, think) about that before but that it [14]........................ (not, be) a problem at all. I really hope that I'll get this exciting job and be able to start working as an event manager soon!"

nach SB p. 51

Worksheet 4

■ 1 **Look at the pictures. Then complete the sentences with the past or past perfect form of the verbs.**

1 She .... (rush) to the supermarket because she .... (forget) to buy some milk.

2 He .... (feel) sick because he .... (drink) too much cola.

3 She .... (can, not, find) her sandwich because her dog .... (steal) it out of her school bag in the morning.

4 She .... (must, sit) down because she .... (eat) too much of her birthday cake.

5 He .... (can, not, sleep) because he .... (not, eat) anything for dinner. So he .... (get) some cornflakes from the kitchen.

6 After he .... (work) out at the gym, they .... (go) to a restaurant.

Worksheet 1

● 1 **Complete the sentences with the adjective or adverb.**

Superman is probably the best-known superhero. He grew up in a [1].. (small) town in America and then came to the [2].. (big) city of Metropolis to work for The Daily Planet, a newspaper. There he met his girlfriend, Lois Lane, and later they were [3].. (happy) married.

Superman has lots of superpowers: He can fly [4]...................................... (quick) from one place to the next. He isn't only very [5]... (fast), he's also very [6]... (strong). What's more, he has X-ray eyes and can see through things. He can always see everything very [7]... (clear). He also has a really [8]... (good) memory and can hear voices [9]... (perfect) from a great distance. He has adventures with some very [10]... (evil) and [11]... (dangerous) characters, like Lex Luthor, Doomsday and Bizarro. He fights against them [12]... (brave) and in the end Superman wins. He is always stronger and cleverer than them.

■ 2 **Circle the correct option, either the adjective or adverb.**

Here is what the chef Sam Reed says about food and a healthy diet:

"Nutritious food can be prepared [1] **quick / quickly**. Just buy some fresh meat or fish, add some fresh vegetables, and some potatoes or rice. It's really [2] **easy / easily** to eat well and not have junk food all the time. All you need are the right ingredients. Compared to a cooked meal, junk food doesn't only taste [3] **bad / badly**, it also has [4] **harmful / harmfully** effects on your body. You should always decide [5] **careful / carefully** what you eat and what is [6] **good / well** for your health. Always eat [7] **slow / slowly**. Then you won't get fat [8] **easy / easily** and you'll always stay [9] **active / actively**!"

nach SB p. 52

Worksheet 2

★ 1 a **Look at the pictures. Then write part 2 of the story "Nightmare over the city". Use the characters from the Student's Book again:**

Nightmare over the city – Part 2

Superkid / Matt Kidevil Morgan Janet Monday

★ b **Now write an ending of about 100 – 120 words for your story.**

Worksheet 3

■ 1 **Have another look at the lyrics of the song *Superman* by *R.E.M.* (Student's Book p. 55). Imagine that you are talking to the boy in the song. Complete the sentences with the correct question tags.**

1 "You are Superman, ...?"

2 "And you always know what's happening, ...?"

3 "Your girlfriend doesn't really love that guy, ...?"

4 "And he isn't really interested in her, ...? He's just playing games, ...?"

5 "You can see right through her and him, ...?"

6 "You will be able to find her even if she's a million miles away, ...?"

7 "One last question: You know that you're dreaming, ...?"

▶ nach SB p. 55

Worksheet 4

1 Read the following biography. Then mark the statements T (*True*) or F (*False*).

Heath Ledger

Heath Ledger (1979 – 2008) was an Australian-born actor who had a lot of success in his career. Already at an early age he loved acting and had his first experiences on stage when he was ten. He then went on to star in smaller roles in Australian TV series and films. Although he had always loved acting, he suffered from stage fright* and did not feel very comfortable when he got too much attention from the media.

During the 1990s he moved to New York City where he further developed his film career. Some of his best-known films include *Ten Things I Hate About You* (1999), *The Patriot* (2000), *Monster's Ball* (2001), in which he played with Halle Berry, *A Knight's Tale* (2001), *Brokeback Mountain* (2005), and *The Dark Knight* (2008).

In 2005 Heath Ledger was nominated* for an Academy Award ("Oscar") for Best Actor for his performance* as a gay ranch worker in *Brokeback Mountain*. On the set of the film he also met Michelle Williams, and they dated for the following two years. The couple had a daughter in 2005.

His next-to-last performance was as The Joker in *The Dark Knight*. With his terrifying white make-up, his ugly red lips and his evil character, The Joker is one of the best-known supervillains in film history. For his fantastic performance as Batman's enemy, Heath Ledger was again nominated for an Academy Award as Best Supporting Actor*. This time he won the award, but tragically, it came too late for him. He was found dead in his New York flat on 22 January 2008. Fans and the media were shocked by his early death at the age of 28. *The Dark Knight* went on to become the most successful film of the year in 2008. His family accepted the Academy Award for him. Heath Ledger has repeatedly been said to be one of the best actors of his generation. He will definitely be remembered for his role as the supervillain The Joker in *The Dark Knight*.

VOCABULARY
stage fright – Lampenfieber
nominate – nominieren
performance – Rolle, Darstellung
Best Supporting Actor – Bester Nebendarsteller (Kategorie bei den Oscars)

		T	F
1	Heath Ledger had his biggest success in Australia.	☐	☐
2	Throughout his career he made a number of films and also played in a movie with Halle Berry.	☐	☐
3	He was nominated for Best Supporting Actor in *Brokeback Mountain*.	☐	☐
4	The actor has a daughter with co-actress Matilda Williams.	☐	☐
5	In *The Dark Knight* he played The Joker, which was also his last role in his short life.	☐	☐
6	The Academy Award was accepted by members of his family after his death.	☐	☐

Worksheet I

● 1 **Use the present simple for future to write Amy's travel blog.**

1 We (be) off to Australia at nine p.m. on Friday.

....

2 Our plane (arrive) at 00.30 on Sunday.

....

3 On the third day, our plane to Alice Springs (leave) at 8.30 a.m.

....

4 Mum, dad, Ryan and me, we (climb) the Sydney Harbour Bridge at 8.30 a.m.

....

5 We (fly) back to London at five p.m.

....

6 Our plane (touch) down at London Heathrow airport at seven a.m.

....

★ 2 **Read about Eve's and Jeremy's adventure (Student's Book p. 60) again. Back home in Great Britain, Eve and Jeremy were interviewed by a reporter about it. Write the interview for a travel magazine.**

E = Eve **J** = Jeremy **R** = reporter

R: Eve and Jeremy, it's been a week now since your return from your trip to Australia. Can you tell us a bit about your holidays?

E: Of course. Australia is just an amazing country. If you love being outdoors and enjoy the wildlife, it's the perfect place for your holidays. The people are so friendly there, and very relaxed. As a tourist you should listen to their advice; they know their country best.

J: Eve's right. A man at the tourist office in Broome told us that it might be dangerous to camp near the Pentecost River. There had been lots of stories about aggressive crocodiles.

R: But you didn't listen to him, did you?

Continue. Use the information from the Student's Book.

  ▶ nach SB p. 61

Worksheet 2

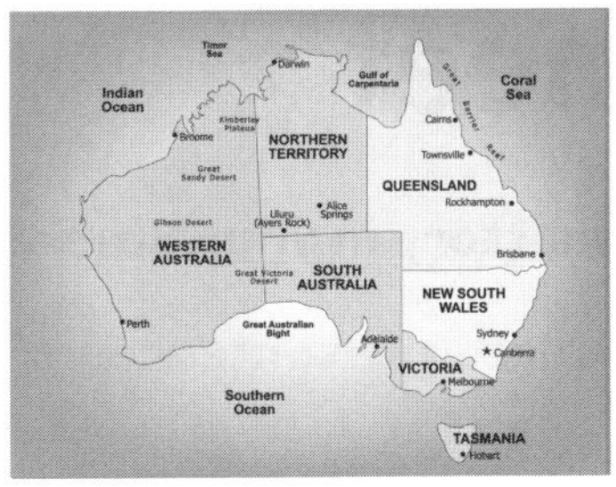

★ **1 Write Rick's travel blog.**

Rick is spending his holidays in Australia with his parents. Look at the information boxes about the places he has visited so far. Then write about his adventures in his blog. Also mention how he got from one place to the next.

Mataranka Hot Springs

walk through the forest
took a bath in hot springs: 32°C, flying foxes* and spiders in the trees above our heads

the great barrier reef

trip in glass-bottom boat*: saw coral reefs*, lots of beautiful fish, sea turtles*
scuba diving in the afternoon: exciting trip, took lots of photos

ALICE SPRINGS

tour of the old town
two-day trip to Redbank Gorge*: with Aborigine guide, set up camp, campfire, tried to play the didgeridoo

Kakadu National Park

guided 4x4 tour, stop at waterfalls
lots of animals: kangaroos, wallabies*, saltwater crocodiles in billabongs*

VOCABULARY
glass-bottom boat – Boot mit gläsernem Boden
coral reef – Korallenriff
sea turtle – Meeresschildkröte
wallaby – kleine Känguru-Art
billabong – Tümpel, kleiner Teich
flying fox – Flughund
gorge – Schlucht, Klamm

Days 3 and 4: We've finally arrived at the Great Barrier Reef. What a great place for a holiday! In the morning, we went to the beach and booked a tour on board a glass-bottom boat. …

Worksheet 3

■ 1 **Read the story in your Student's Book (p. 62) again.**

a Complete the sentences with adjective or adverb.

When the Aborigine told him [1].. (excited) about the men at the bar, the bank manager decided to see Inspector Saunders [2].. (quick). The inspector listened to his story [3].. (quiet). Then he told him, "This doesn't sound [4].. (good). It's almost [5].. (impossible) to get to Wilcannia [6].. (safe). The sun is so [7].. (hot) and the ground is extremely [8].. (dry)." The manager said, "I [9].. (complete) agree with you, but the men are [10].. (dangerous). Help me, please!" So Saunders sent for an Aboriginal tracker who would help him on the [11].. (difficult) journey. They thought of a [12].. (clever) plan. They planned very [13].. (careful) and only travelled by night to protect themselves and their horses from the heat. On the last day of their journey, they [14].. (sudden) heard a noise. They met two men who were too [15].. (weak) to speak.

b Read the sentences below and write a different ending to the story.

The two men were very thirsty and couldn't walk. Saunders gave them some water when suddenly they heard a shot. "What's that?" he thought. He turned around and …*

VOCABULARY
shot – Schuss

....

....

....

....

....

....

....

....

....

▶ nach SB p. 63

Worksheet 4

■ 1 a **Read Addie's text about her life in the outback and the school she goes to. Then answer the questions.**

Hi, my name's Addie, and I live on a "station", that's a sheep farm in the central outback of Australia, with my parents and my two younger brothers. The nearest town is Alice Springs, which is more than 300 km away from my home. Two or three times each year everyone meets up in Alice Springs and I travel to school there to see my teachers and classmates for a week. Normally my classroom is the living room on our farm and I take part in my classes on the Internet. That sounds strange to you, doesn't it? Now let me explain a bit about my school, the Alice Springs School of the Air. When I started school eight years ago, I had my first lessons over the radio. Each day I had one lesson with my teacher on the radio and lots of homework to do. My parents helped me with the homework in the beginning; my mum taught me how to read and to write. With the Internet, things are a lot easier now. I send my homework by email to my teachers. The online lessons are much more fun than being on the radio and they offer lots of activities with my classmates. We can see each other through a webcam, we have our own students' website and we chat online each day. My parents told me what school was like for them when they were young. They both also grew up in the outback and didn't go to a school building either. They had to send in their homework using the Flying Doctors Services. Can you imagine that, a pilot picking up your homework? The radio classes started in 1951, so my grandparents went to the School of the Air, too. Back then there were often a lot of problems and there was no school for many days. The Alice Springs School of the Air has about 160 students (aged 5 to 14) at the moment and covers an area of 1,300,000 km^2. So you could say that I go to the "world's largest classroom" – and I'm proud of it. At the moment I'm looking for new friends from all over the world. I'm really interested in other countries and would like to learn about your school life, so please drop me a line. Send in your emails and say hi!

1 Where does Addie live?

....

2 How far away is the nearest school?

....

3 When does she meet her teachers and classmates?

....

4 How does she contact her teachers and her classmates?

....

5 How did her parents' teachers get the students' homework?

....

6 Why does she go to the world's largest classroom?

....

★ b **Write an email of about 120 – 150 words to Addie and tell her about a typical day at your school. Write about:**

- how long it takes you to get to school;
- what lessons you like most/least;
- why you would/wouldn't like to go to the School of the Air.

▶ nach SB p. **63**

Worksheet I

1 a What *might* / *may* / *could* happen in these countries if ...? If you can't remember the missing details, look at your Student's Book (p. 70) again.

Example:

1 If you show your feet or shoes in Thailand, people / think / that ...

If you show your feet or shoes in Thailand, people might think that you want to insult them.

2 Japanese people / smile / if ...

....

....

3 People in the Middle and Far East / think / that you are unclean if you ...

....

4 It / get / you into trouble to use the gesture that means "OK" in ...

....

5 It / not be / a good idea to use the same gesture in France because ...

....

6 People in Japan / not feel / comfortable if you ...

....

7 In Greece or Bulgaria people / take / a "yes" for a "no" if you ...

....

★ **b Now do some more research on the Internet about different customs* in different cultures. Here are some further questions:**

1 In which country do people show their tongues when they greet members of their family and friends?
2 How often do French people kiss each other's cheeks when they meet?
3 In which country is it a common custom to wash the guest's feet as a greeting?

Answer these questions. Then try to find out about two more customs and write sentences about them.

VOCABULARY
custom – Brauch

....

....

....

....

....

....

....

Worksheet 2

1 Read the presentation that Lawrence gives at school about goth culture. Then answer the questions below.

"Good morning everybody! Today I'd like to give a presentation on goth subculture and how it began. I started to wear goth clothes a year ago and some of my friends are into the goth trend, too.

The goth subculture can be found in many different countries around the world today. It began in Great Britain during the early 1980s when it developed out of the punk scene, which was a popular trend in the 1970s. Now goth subculture has many different forms. Historically, the word goth goes back to the Goths who were a German people from the East and played an important role in early European history. The term Gothic* can also be found in architecture. In the late 1700s people became interested in ancient Gothic buildings in Great Britain. This then gave birth to a new literary movement* in the 19th century, the Gothic movement. In Gothic novels you will often find a love of strange, dark things, horror and the supernatural*. People interested in goth culture like castles, churches, ghosts and vampires. Characters like Dracula or Frankenstein's monster go back to that time.

The goth subculture has special tastes in music and clothes. Some early goth bands, for example, were *Siouxsie and the Banshees*, *The Cure*, and *The Sisters of Mercy*. Black clothes and large crosses worn around the neck, dyed black hair and lots of dark make-up are typical of what goths like to wear. Many young people who are goths are often mistaken for violent and aggressive teenagers because of their black clothes and white faces. However, the opposite is often true. Most of them are very quiet and rather tolerant people. They just want to express that they are special and different. And this, of course, goes for me, too.

After 30 years, the goth movement continues to grow, and has become one of today's longest surviving youth subcultures."

VOCABULARY
Gothic – Gotik, gotisch
literary movement – Literaturbewegung
the supernatural – das Übernatürliche

1 When did the goth subculture start?

....

2 Historically, where did the word come from?

....

3 What can be found in Gothic literature?

....

4 What do goths usually wear?

....

5 What do goths want to express with the way they look?

....

Worksheet 3

★ 1 **Read the text and do the exercise(s).**

The new tattoo

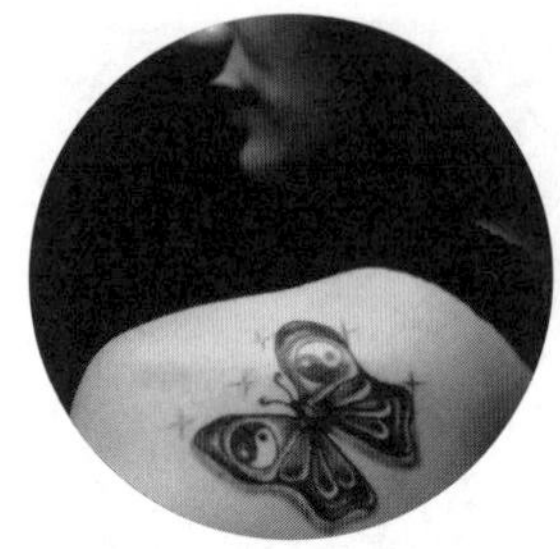

Three days ago Amanda, 14, went to a tattoo studio. She has wanted to get a tattoo for a long time and has saved all her money for the past two years. Now she has a butterfly tattooed on her left shoulder. She told the man at the tattoo studio that she was already 17 because she didn't have her mother's permission to get a tattoo. He didn't seem to care.

The next day at school she showed her best friend Sharon her new tattoo. Sharon said that she liked the tattoo but she couldn't understand why Amanda hadn't asked her mother for her permission. Now Amanda is afraid that her mum might find out. She thinks she will be really angry at her. But doesn't Amanda have a right to decide for herself?

a Amanda doesn't know what to do and writes a letter to an Agony Aunt. Write Amanda's letter of 120 – 160 words.

- Explain why you got the tattoo;
- write about Sharon's reaction;
- ask for advice: how to explain the situation to your mother.
  What might your mum say?

b Write the Agony Aunt's answer to Amanda's letter in 120 – 150 words.

■ 2 **Read the leaflet. Then write a comment of about 100 – 120 words in which you say why you would / wouldn't be interested in it.**

Worksheet 4

■ **1 Look at the pictures. What *might* / *may* / *could* happen next? Use a word from the box for each situation to write a sentence.**

win | blow away | miss | ~~fall off~~ | attack | buy | fall asleep

1

He might fall off the ladder.

....

2

The shark ....

....

3

The girl ....

....

4

She ....

....

5

He ....

....

6

The storm ....

....

7

She ....

....

Worksheet I

UNIT 10

■ 1 **Read the texts about people's collections. Whose collection do you like most? Choose one person. Then write an interview of about 120 – 150 words with her/him. Use the following questions in the interview. Make up two more questions and her/his answers.**

Strange collections

Marcia, 32: I collect tickets. I've got a huge collection of more than 900 tickets. I keep all kinds of tickets, bus, train and plane tickets, cinema tickets, theatre tickets, concert tickets, etc. I stick them in books and write the date next to the ticket. The oldest ticket in my collection is a bus ticket which I bought at the age of eight. That's when I had the idea to start a collection. My collection helps me remember the places and events I've been to. Sometimes I take out my books and look through them. Some of my friends think that I'm a bit crazy, but I love my hobby and I will continue collecting a lot more tickets in the future.

Donald, 14: I collect pucks. I have played in an ice hockey team for two years now. From October to April we always have a game at the weekends. We also go to other cities to play the other teams. I try to keep a puck from each game. Sometimes I also buy one at souvenir shops. Now members of my family and friends have started to bring back pucks from other countries, too. My aunt gave me the most precious puck in my collection; she brought it back from the Olympic Winter Games as a souvenir. It's a Canadian puck, and the Canadians won gold in the Olympic ice hockey competition. I'm really proud of it. Until now, I've collected 92 pucks.

Natasha, 17: I collect dreams. I once read an article about a woman who had collected dreams for all her life. I was so fascinated by her story that I decided to start my own dream collection. I keep a dream diary on my bedside table. First thing in the morning, I write about my dream in my diary. I'm very good at remembering my dreams. I've collected 673 dreams so far. Some of my friends also got interested in my hobby. So in my dream diary there is a special part for my friends. Whenever they have a funny, unusual or exciting dream, they write it down for me and I add their stories to my dream journal.

What do you collect?
When did you start your collection?
Why is your collection important to you?
How many have you got?
What do your friends say about your hobby?
How long will you continue collecting?

nach SB p. 76

Worksheet 2

■ 1 **Read the text. Choose the correct word for each space from the box.**

1 favourite – illegal – strange
2 looked at – broke into – searched for
3 most expensive – rarest – most unusual
4 fined – questioned – taken to prison
5 find – check out – take
6 good – famous – experienced
7 already – just – almost
8 of – by – from

Yesterday Colin Watson, 63, climbed his last tree. The man was known to the police and the RSPB (The Royal Society for the Protection of Birds) for his [1].. hobby. Mr Watson had started his hobby as a schoolboy. He became the biggest collector of wild birds' eggs in Great Britain. When officers of the RSPB [2].. his collection at his house some years ago, they found more than 2,000 eggs. The [3].. eggs in his collection were those of the golden eagle. Watson was arrested and [4]... many times.

Yesterday afternoon he wanted to [5]... another bird's nest. The [6].. collector climbed a 12-metre high tree. Because of the very strong wind he fell out of the tree onto the hard ground. When the ambulance arrived soon afterwards, it was [7]... too late. He died at the scene [8]... his injuries. It was a tragic accident, but what he did to the birds was also a tragedy. Now Colin Watson's collection will be moved from his house to the RSPB.

Worksheet 3

■ 1 **Complete the dialogue with the correct tense (present perfect or past simple).**

An interview with Marcela T., who owns an unusual collection of tea bags.

I=Interviewer, **M**=Marcela

I: Marcela, can you tell me about your unusual collection? What do you collect?

M: Yes, of course. I collect tea bags.

I: Tea bags ... that's interesting. When did you get the idea for your hobby?

M: Well, five years ago I 1 .... (spend) a holiday in England with my husband. One afternoon, we 2 .... (go) to this lovely tea house and 3 .... (have) some tea. When the waiter 4 .... (bring) some hot water and a box with lots of different tea bags in it, I 5 .... (start) to study them carefully. That's when I 6 .... (know) that I 7 .... (want) to start a collection.

I: And how many tea bags 8 .... (you, collect) so far?

M: I 9 .... (collect) more than 500 now.

I: 10 .... (you, buy) all the tea bags?

M: I 11 .... (buy) some of them but I also 12 .... (ask) my friends to bring tea bags back from their holidays. My best friend Antonia 13 .... (just, give) me this beautiful bag here, a bag of white tea from China.

I: How long will you continue your collection?

M: I really don't know, but tea bags 14 .... (not, lose) their fascination for me yet. I'm still happy about each new bag in my collection. And I'm also thinking about buying a cupboard where I can put them on display*. Right now I keep them in wooden boxes in the kitchen.

I: Thank you, it was very interesting to talk to you.

VOCABULARY
put on display – ausstellen

  ▶ nach SB p. **80**

Worksheet 4

■ **1 Read the text. Then fill in the correct tense (present perfect or past simple).**

"It [1]................................ (be) my cousin's wedding last weekend. Mum, dad and me, we [2]................................ (fly) to Liverpool on Friday evening and [3]................................ (stay) at Uncle Jack's and Aunt Nancy's place for the weekend. My cousin Joy [4]................................ (know) Stuart, her husband, for some years now. They [5]................................ (meet) each other in 2007. [6]................................ (I, tell) you about my uncle yet? Well, I think he's really embarrassing. He's always making fun of me and the way I look, but he's the only one laughing about his jokes! But it was Joy's wedding and she [7]................................ (ask) me to be her bridesmaid, so I [8]................................ (must) laugh at his silly jokes and admire her awful ugly wedding dress. The wedding was really nice and Joy and Stuart both looked so happy. When I finally [9]................................ (change) into my black clothes, I [10]................................ (feel) much better. And there [11]................................ (be) this boy who had changed into his goth clothes too – Lawrence, Stuart's cousin. I [12]................................ (never, meet) anyone as interesting as him. He's just so cool and we [13]................................ (have) a lot of fun that night. After the party he [14]................................ (promise) to contact me again. Since last weekend, I [15]................................ (spend) hours in front of the computer chatting with him and he [16]................................ (already, send) me lots of emails with photos of the place where he lives in London. I can hardly wait to see him again!"

■ **2 Read what Katia, the girl from Austria who visited her penfriend Jessica in England, told The Mag and circle the correct tense.**

"[1] **I travelled / I've travelled** to Great Britain many times before because my mum is English and my grandparents live here. [2] **I wore / I've worn** my boots for three months now; your headmaster [3] **was / has been** the first to object to them. Yesterday he [4] **told / has told** me that I [5] **wasn't / haven't been** allowed to wear them to school. [6] **I talked / I've talked** to two girls in the cafeteria yesterday afternoon. They [7] **said / have said** that they [8] **liked / have liked** my boots and that they [9] **weren't / haven't been** too happy about their school uniforms. [10] **I never had / I've never had** any problems with the way I dress at my school. So I'm glad when I'm back and I can put on my boots again."

etwas ablehnen

Worksheet I

1 Complete the sentences with the correct form of the 1st and 2nd Conditional.

Juanita Carlos works very hard for little money. Here is what she says:

1 I wouldn't get more money if I .... (work) harder.

2 If it .... (go) on like that, I will always have a poor life.

3 If coffee prices .... (be) better, I wouldn't be so worried.

4 If I earned more money, I .... (buy) a car and a TV for my family.

5 I .... (sell) my farm and we .... (move) to the city if I find a buyer.

6 If I could afford* it, I .... (send) my children to a good school.

VOCABULARY
afford sth – sich etwas leisten

2 Complete the sentences with the correct form of the 3rd Conditional.

Ramon Machado works on a coffee farm in Honduras. He takes part in a Fair Trade project. Here is what he says:

1 If I .... (know) more about Fair Trade some years ago, I would have joined earlier.

2 If a friend of mine hadn't told me about the Fair Trade project, I .... (not, ask) to join it.

3 If it hadn't been for Fair Trade, I .... (not, have) enough money to keep my farm.

4 If they .... (not, pay) me a fixed price, I wouldn't have been able to pay my bills.

5 I .... (use) pesticides if Fair trade hadn't shown me other ways of farming.

6 My children wouldn't have had the chance to go to school if I .... (continue) working on my own.

  ▶ nach SB p. 82

Worksheet 2

■ 1 **Read the text. Then complete the fact sheet.**

Nuts from Brazil – another Fair Trade project

Brazil nuts* only grow in certain areas of the Amazon rainforest (Bolivia, Brazil, Peru). The trees grow up to 50 metres tall and live for up to 1,000 years. Each tree produces up to 1,300 grapefruit-sized pods* which have 20 to 40 nuts in each of them. The pods drop to the forest floor when it rains between January and March. They are collected by nut gatherers* who fill bags weighing up to 70 kg which they carry on their backs along narrow paths through the rainforest.

The Amazon has a lot of problems today and losing trees from the rainforest is one of the biggest and most dangerous. Nut collecting plays an important role in helping to save the rainforest. Nut gatherers are farmers who earn money without cutting down trees. They get a fair price for the nuts from a Fair Trade project in the area. The Fair Trade partners sell the nuts to other organisations. In the last few years, about 19,000 tons of nuts were exported to other countries.

VOCABULARY
Brazil nut – Paranuss
pod – Schale
gatherer – Sammler/in

Fact sheet

Brazil nuts grow in 1 ....

The trees grow up to 2 .... metres and live for up to 3 ....

Each tree produces up to 4 .... pods with 5 .... nuts.

The pods drop to the floor during the 6 ....

The nuts are collected by gatherers who carry up to 7 .... on their backs.

8 .... is one of the biggest problems in the Amazon.

Nut collecting helps to 9 .... the rainforest because the trees 10 .... down.

Fair Trade guarantees a 11 .... for the nuts.

About 12 .... of nuts were exported in the last few years.

Worksheet 3

★ **1** **Imagine the following situation: Your friend who comes from another country is being bullied and attacked by other kids at school. They make fun of the way she/he looks and play nasty tricks on her/him. Only yesterday they insulted her/him, called her/him awful names and took away her/his Maths homework.**

a Write an email of about 130 – 180 words and tell another friend about the situation.

- Say what happened at school.
- Tell her/him about your feelings.
- Ask for her/his advice.

b Then write your friend's answer to your email (120 – 150 words).

★ **2** **Choose one of the sentences below. Then write a story about a situation in which the main character of your story felt that way (150 – 200 words). Find a good title for your story.**

"I'm so terribly annoyed!"

"I was really shocked."

"I've never been so frustrated before."

- Describe what happened and when it happened.
- Write about the people who were involved.
- Explain what the main character of your story decided to do.

....

....

....

....

....

....

....

....

....

Worksheet 4

★ 1 **Complete the sentences about people from your Student's Book with the 3rd Conditional of the verbs in brackets.**

1 Isabel Miller wouldn't have murdered John Murdoch if he .... (leave) his wife.

2 If Stevie hadn't left the garden party without a word, Rachel .... (feel) much better.

3 If the young girls .... (not, say) that the people of Salem were witches, they wouldn't have been executed.

4 If Mandy hadn't joined the junior cadets at the age of 13, she .... (not, have) the idea to become a soldier.

5 Many people in Great Britain .... (not, hear) anything about healthy nutrition if Jamie Oliver hadn't started the Feed Me Better movement.

6 If Superkid had found the machine earlier, Morgan .... (not, take) the sleeping pills.

7 Eve and Jeremy wouldn't have been attacked by a crocodile if they .... (not, be) camping near the Pentecost River.

8 If Colin Watson had been more careful when he climbed the tree, he .... (not, fall) to death.

Worksheet 1

■ 1 **Read the book reports. Then do the tasks on Worksheet 2.**

1

Forever in Blue: The Fourth Summer of the Sisterhood

Author: Ann Brashares

What's it about?

In the fourth novel of *The Sisterhood of the Traveling Pants** series, the four friends Lena, Bridget, Tibby, and Carmen are at different universities and beginning to experience different things in their lives. Lena, Bridget and Tibby have problems with their boyfriends and families. Carmen moves on to become an actress. The traveling pants, which were so important in the three earlier books of the series, disappear. These magic pants, which fit all of the girls although they are different sizes, have been passed on between them and are the magical link in their friendship.

Now Effie, Lena's younger sister, steals them and takes them with her to Greece where she accidentally loses them. The four friends decide to travel to Greece to look for the pants. They enjoy spending time together and realise that they haven't been together for over a year. But will they find the pants? How can their friendship continue without them?

What do I think of it?

I really liked reading about the four girls and their lives. They are so different, but in the end they always get together and manage to keep up their friendship. Several unexpected things happen in the book and the ending is really surprising, too.

All in all, I would say that it is a good and easy read but it definitely helps to know the other books in the series. Then you won't be disappointed. And I'd recommend it for girls rather than boys because it is easier for girls to understand the four friends' problems.

VOCABULARY
traveling pants (AE) – „Hose auf Wanderschaft"

2

The Curious Incident of the Dog in the Night-Time

Author: Mark Haddon

What's it about?

The story is told by Christopher Francis Boone, a 15-year-old boy who suffers from autism*, an illness you'll learn a lot about in the book. He lives with his father. One day, he finds the neighbour's dog dead in the garden. He wants to try and solve the case and investigate the dog's death, so he starts to write a murder mystery novel. Lots of things happen as Christopher finds out the truth about the people close to him and as he sets off on an adventurous journey. In the end, he returns to Swindon, where he now lives with his mother and is very optimistic about his future – he gets an A in his A-level Maths and wants to become a scientist.

What do I think of it?

This is clearly one of the best books I've ever read. It's exciting and full of surprises. I learned a lot about autism because the story is told by Christopher himself. It's amazing how he manages the difficult situations in his life. He is also a mathematical genius and you'll read about his special talents. If you're interested in detective novels, it's definitely a book for you.

VOCABULARY
autism – Autismus

Worksheet 2

■ 1 **Match the novels with these types of books from Worksheet 1.**

thriller	....
detective	....
fantasy	....
historical novel	....
adventure	....
science fiction	....
young adult novel	....

■ 2 **Read the sentences. Tick T (*True*) or F (*False*).**

	T	F
1 The four friends in *The Sisterhood of the Traveling Pants* have a lot in common.	☐	☐
2 They haven't seen each other for some time when they get together in Greece.	☐	☐
3 The writer of the book report thinks that you should read the other books in the series before reading *Forever in Blue: The Fourth Summer of the Sisterhood.*	☐	☐
4 Christopher asks a detective to find out why the neighbour's dog died.	☐	☐
5 Christopher is interested in Science.	☐	☐
6 He writes a novel about a murder and is excellent at Maths.	☐	☐

■ 3 **If you had to choose, which of the two books would you like to read and why? Write a short paragraph and give reasons (80 – 100 words).**

....

....

....

....

....

....

....

....

....

Worksheet 3

■ **1** **Ask a classmate / a friend about what he/she likes reading. Here are some questions. Add two more and write down the answers.**

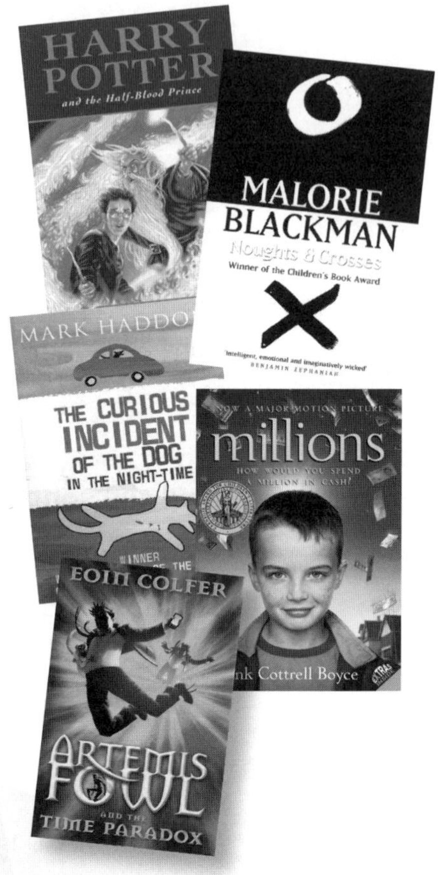

Do you like reading? Why / why not?

Would you call yourself a "book person"? Why / why not?

What is your favourite book? Why?

What was your favourite story / book when you were younger?

What is the best book you've ever read for school?

What is it about?

Why did you enjoy reading it?

■ **2** **Now answer the questions for yourself and write a text about what you like reading. (150 – 200 words).**

★ **3** **Think of a book you've recently read. Write a letter to the author of the book. In your letter, tell her/him:**

- if it was an easy read for you;
- why you read the book (for school/for yourself);
- what you liked/didn't like about the book (characters, storyline, etc.);
- what you would have changed in the book.

Worksheet 4

■ **1 Read the text about a camping trip. Fill in the missing reflexive pronouns.**

Two weeks ago, Louise, Paul, Karen and I went camping. We stayed at a campsite near Snakeriver Forest. Lots of things went wrong on our trip. We didn't enjoy [1]............................ there. I'd never been camping before so I couldn't put up the tent [2]............................ .The others were annoyed and told me, "You should be able to do it [3]............................, we can't do everything for you." When we went for a hike, Louise fell and hurt [4]............................ . Her left ankle was swollen badly, so we had to return to the campsite. We could only walk slowly because of her injury. Then we were really hungry and wanted to prepare a barbecue, but Paul cut [5]............................ with a knife. He was terribly white in the face. When he felt better, he went to the nearest shop with Karen. There they bought [6]............................ some sandwiches and ice cream but they didn't buy anything for Louise and me. That's when I started asking [7]............................ why I had joined them on this trip.

★ **2 Complete the sentences with the words in the box and a reflexive pronoun.**

read
got
call
look after
write
enjoy

1 They should get a babysitter. Leonie can't ....
2 Jenny and Sharif, did you .... at the party?
3 He didn't copy from his neighbour. He .... the story ....
4 If you want to know how the book continues, you'll have to .... it ....
5 We don't know where we are and it's getting dark. I think we .... into trouble.
6 I wouldn't .... an expert in history, but I've read lots of books about the Middle Ages.

Worksheet 1

UNIT 13

★ 1 **Max is spending a holiday in Florida. He is staying in a hotel near Cape Canaveral, close to the Kennedy Space Center. Read through the notes he took about his trip. Then write Max's email to a friend (130 – 180 words).**

In the email, you tell her/him
- about the exciting things you've already seen/done
- about the things you're going to do tomorrow
- about your plan to become an astronaut.

arrived yesterday – went on a guided tour
museum + Rocket Garden: real space shuttles, huge
best part of visit: simulation inside a space shuttle
wore a space suit
countdown and take-off

evening: to the IMAX cinema: film about the history of space travel –
want to be an astronaut, too!

tomorrow:
interview with a retired astronaut at the Kennedy Space Center,
have lots of questions,
very excited!

....

....

....

....

....

....

....

....

....

....

....

....

Worksheet 2

■ 1 **Read the ending of the story *The Price* from your Student's Book (pp. 100/101).**

It was Emily's most perfect picture ever – an alien spaceship taking off from Earth. Emily's father looked at the picture more closely. There at the door was a teenage girl. It was Emily. Emily's father and mother looked at each other. They knew she was never coming back.

Emily was gone. But every day in the morning, there was a message from Emily to her parents on the desk in her room. Here are the first messages she sent to them:

Day 1

Dear Mum and Dad,

Don't worry about me! I'm really fine, I just need to get away for a while. My friends from outer space have asked me for help. I'm travelling to their planet and will be gone for a few days.

E.

Day 2

Dear Mum and Dad,

I'm still on the spaceship. About 50 aliens are travelling with me. They're all very friendly. I'm looking at the Earth from above; it's beautiful! I wish I had my camera with me to take some photos. The food's really good, I can choose from lots of different meals they've prepared for me. So you see, there's really no need to worry.

Love, E.

Day 3

Dear Mum and Dad,

We've finally arrived after a long, long journey. I've always wanted to come here and visit my friends on their planet. I've been to other planets before, but this one's just amazing. Mum, do you remember the day when you found the paintings in my room? It looks exactly like my pictures. There are lots of exotic flowers and strange animals living in huge forests. And the planet has three suns. I have to finish now. My friends are coming to see me. They want to discuss a problem. I wonder what it is. I hope I'll be able to help them!

Bye, E.

Write two more letters (about 100 words each). Before you write the letters, think of the following:

- What is the problem the aliens tell her about?
- How does she solve this problem?
- Does she enjoy her stay on the planet?
- When and how does she travel back to Earth?

Worksheet 3

★ **1** **Look at the ad. Then complete the sentences with the correct form of the phrasal verbs in the box.**

Reach for the stars and travel to space!!!

✓ Spend a week at an astronauts' training center* in the United States.
✓ Go on a special training seminar with our experts (space suits included).
✓ Go on a 40-minute trip into space on our rocket plane XY, 100 km above the earth!
✓ Enjoy our after-flight party!

This is a wonderful experience!
Special offer – only $330,000!
Contact us now!

run out of wait for take off look at come up with set off return to earth turn into

Last week the travel agency* Spacefly [1].. a fantastic new idea. They invited people on a trip into space! Lots of people [2]...................................... the exciting ad on TV and read about the special offer in newspapers and magazines. They will get special training at a space center in America. At the end of the week they will [3]...................................... in a rocket plane and travel 100 km above the earth.

The trip will last up to 40 minutes. The rocket plane will be comfortable and the agency promises that it won't [4].. fuel. When the rocket plane [5]... after the trip, there will be a party for the "astronauts".

The travel agency also promises to [6]......................... this trip .... a wonderful experience. Some people called the agency immediately. They just couldn't [7]................................. their journey to start and wanted to [8]...................................... for the USA straightaway.

There is only one problem: the first rocket plane will not be ready for take-off until the year 2025!

VOCABULARY
center (AE) – centre (BE)
travel agency – Reiseagentur

Worksheet 4

● 1 **Circle the correct words.**

1 Go ahead, Fido! Get the ball! What are you waiting **on / for**?

2 I can't come to the cinema with you tonight. I spent all my pocket money **on / for** CDs.

3 Yesterday we went to the museum where a guide took us on a tour. We looked **after / at** a lot of famous paintings.

4 At the ice cream parlour you can choose **from / between** 100 different kinds of ice cream.

5 They blew **up / off** lots of colourful balloons and hung them all up in the garden for his birthday party.

6 They lost their yacht last summer. It hit some rocks and broke **up / off** in a storm.

■ 2 **Write the sentences again and use a phrasal verb for the underlined part of the sentence.**

Example:

<u>We don't have any milk any more</u>, I'm going to the supermarket to get some.

We have run out of milk, I'm going to the supermarket to get some.

1 As <u>the plane left the ground</u>, she took lots of photos of the city.

....

2 <u>She doesn't have a good relationship with him.</u> They always fight.

....

3 Their car stopped because <u>there was no more fuel</u>.

....

4 They didn't know how to get to the next city, but <u>Michael had a really great idea.</u>
He suggested walking!

....

5 We met at the shopping centre and <u>just stayed there for the afternoon, doing nothing</u>.

....

6 In the evening the sky slowly changed colour and <u>day became night</u>.

....

7 Soon after <u>we had started our journey</u>, we realised that we had forgotten to lock the door.
So we returned home.

....

Worksheet 1

UNIT 14

★ 1 **Read the letter from the editor of TeenWorld. Then do the tasks below.**

A letter from the editor

Hi everybody,

Welcome to our new edition of TeenWorld. In this edition you'll find lots of interesting articles about the summer holidays. Thank you for the letters, photos, and travel reports you sent in – thanks to you this edition has become our largest ever.

Take your time as you look through our magazine and have a look at Sarah's report of her stay in Boston, Andy's travel diary from Down Under, or Brian's review of the music festival in Guildford.

Enjoy your holiday and let us know what you're up to this summer – we'd welcome more reports, emails, letters and photos from you!

Wishing you all the best for a fantastic summer,

your TeenWorld team

a Write one of the texts mentioned in the letter from the editor of TeenWorld:

- Sarah's report from Boston or
- Andy's travel diary from Australia or
- Brian's review of a music festival.

Use the information from your Student's Book (Unit 4, Unit 8, Unit 14). Write about 200 words.

■ **b Write to the magazine about your plans for the summer (150 – 180 words).**

- What are you going to do? What are your favourite activities in summer?
- What places are you going to visit this summer?
- Who's coming with you?

■ 2 **Your English-speaking friend has asked you about your ideas for a perfect holiday. Write an email (120 – 150 words) and consider the following points:**

- Where would you go?
  Describe the place(s) in detail.
- Who would join you?
- How long would you stay there?
- What would you do each day?

  nach SB p. 106

Worksheet 2

■ **1 Read Dominic's report about becoming a BBG at Wimbledon. Then do the task below.**

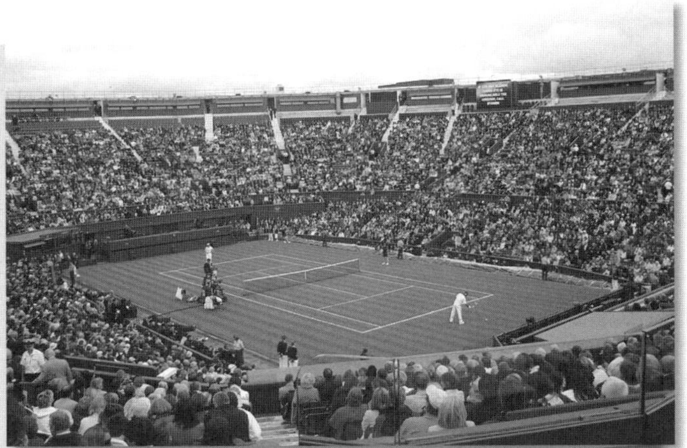

I've always loved sports. I started playing tennis at the age of five. When Tony, who also plays at my tennis club, told me about applying to become a BBG (that's short for a ball boy or girl) at Wimbledon, I decided to join him. I've always wanted to go to Wimbledon and watch the world's top players at this famous tournament. About 400 boys and girls apply each year, but only 200 are chosen in the end. You have to be really fit. The training starts in February and takes place four times a week. It takes a lot of hard work and some of the other boys and girls had to leave because it was simply too much for them. Have you ever tried to run for 12 minutes and then stand completely still for four minutes? This is what we had to do in the first training session and it was really hard. What I liked about the training was that some of the sessions took place inside the All England Lawn Tennis Club and we had a chance to get into the stadium and have a good look around. There's a new museum there with lots of interesting things to see – it's just great for tennis lovers. You can also go on a guided tour and there's even a ghost tour, led by the voice of John McEnroe, one of the greatest players ever. After months of training really hard, I was really happy that I was chosen as a BBG. I'm so excited and can hardly wait for the tournament to start next week. My first match will be a first-round men's doubles. I've heard that the ball can reach speeds of more than 160 kilometres an hour. So I'm definitely going to watch out. I don't want to get hurt. If I do my job really well, there might be a chance to get to the finals. And that has always been my biggest dream.

1 Dominic has always wanted …
- ☐ to join his friend and apply to become a BBG.
- ☐ to see the world's best players at Wimbledon.
- ☐ to become a professional tennis player.
- ☐ to get really fit.

2 The boys and girls who apply …
- ☐ always have training at the All England Tennis Club.
- ☐ have to train four times a week for a year.
- ☐ sometimes have to leave because the training is too hard for them.
- ☐ love going to training in Wimbledon.

3 There is a new museum which …
- ☐ the BBGs visit every day.
- ☐ is where the ghost of John McEnroe lives.
- ☐ offers guided tours to visitors.
- ☐ is full of boring photographs.

4 Dominic is …
- ☐ happy about doing a good job as a BBG.
- ☐ excited about being a BBG in the first round.
- ☐ not worried about getting hurt.
- ☐ unhappy about not being in the finals.

Worksheet 3

■ **1 Write down the opposite of these adjectives.**

1 correct ....
2 fair ....
3 possible ....
4 real ....
5 legal ....
6 responsible ....
7 personal ....
8 healthy ....

★ **2 Complete each sentence with one of the opposites from above.**

1 Too many sweets and too much salt are .... You should eat more vegetables and fruit.

2 You can't get from Vienna to New York in three hours, that's simply ....

3 He's 22 now, but he often acts like a child. I think he needs someone to look after him, he's so ....

4 It's .... to start a campfire* in the forest. You will be arrested if someone finds out about it.

5 They sent me an official invitation to their wedding. I've known them for years, but the text sounds so ....

6 The referee* helped the other team! They won 3:0. It was so ....

7 "I'm sorry, your answer is .... The $200 go to Claire!"

8 The scenes from outer space were so .... in the film that everyone in the cinema started laughing.

VOCABULARY
campfire – Lagerfeuer
referee – Schiedsrichter/in

  ▶ nach SB p. 113

Worksheet 4

■ 1 **Make adjectives from these nouns. Sometimes there are two.**

1 care: ....

2 beauty: ....

3 hope: ....

4 home: ....

5 success: ....

6 meaning: ....

★ 2 **Complete the text with one of the adjectives from above.**

Mrs Davies likes to complain a lot. Here's what she tells a friend on the phone about her neighbour:

"Have you met Bob, my neighbour? Well, it's really difficult to get on with him.

He started his own business in town, but he was so [1]...................................... that the shop had to be shut down.

But he's such a big spender, always wearing the latest fashion and driving expensive cars. If he can't find a new job, he'll end up [2]................................, living in the streets.

What's more, he's such a [3]..................................... driver. He always drives too quickly and never lets people cross the street.

Once he wrote a book of poetry! He gave me a copy, but his poems were just [4]................................ .

There was absolutely nothing in them at all.

Although he isn't friendly or polite himself, his girlfriend is a very nice person.

She's very [5]................................ and has got long black hair.

It's really [6].. – he won't change! I've given up talking to him."